D0492105

Published for Chappel Galleries
by Sansom & Company Ltd, 81g Pembroke Road, Bristol BS8 3EA

April 2002

ISBN 1 900178 49 4

Photographs of the work by Doug Atfield
except "You who live secure in your warm houses . . ." 1994 Courtesy Gainsborough's House, Sudbury, Suffolk
Untitled 1994

Cover: "At the Lido"

Printed by Alphaprint (Colchester) Ltd

15 Colchester Road, Chappel, Essex CO6 2DE
Tele and fax: +44 (0)1206 240326

. . . the parables of sunlight . . .

MARY GRIFFITHS RCA

with an introduction by David Buckman

A Chappel Galleries Monograph

It was my thirtieth year to heaven
Woke to my hearing from harbour and neighbour wood
And the mussell pooled and the heron
Priested shore
The morning beckon
With water praying and call of seagull and rook
And the knock of sailing boats on the net webbed wall
Myself to set foot
That second
In the still sleeping town and set forth.

My birthday began with the water-
Birds and the birds of the winged trees flying my name
Above the farms and the white horses
And I rose
In rainy autumn
And walked abroad in a shower of all my days.
High tide and the heron dived when I took the road
Over the border
And the gates
Of the town closed as the town awoke.

A springful of larks in a rolling
Cloud and the roadside bushes brimming with whistling
Blackbirds and the sun of October
Summery
On the hill's shoulder,
Here were fond climates and sweet singers suddenly
Come in the morning where I wandered and listened
To the rain wringing
Wind blow cold
In the wood faraway under me.

Pale rain over the dwindling harbour
And over the sea wet church the size of a snail
With its horns through mist and the castle
Brown as owls
But all the gardens
Of spring and summer were blooming in the tall tales
Beyond the border and under the lark full cloud.
There could I marvel
My birthday
Away but the weather turned around.

It turned away from the blithe country
And down the other air and the blue altered sky
Streamed again a wonder of summer
With apples
Pears and red currants
And I saw in the turning so clearly a child's
Forgotten mornings when he walked with his mother
Through the parables
Of sun light
And the legends of the green chapels.

And the twice told fields of infancy
That his tears burned my cheeks and his heart moved in mine.
These were the woods the river and sea
Where a boy
In the listening
Summertime of the dead whispered the truth of his joy
To the trees and the stones and the fish in the tide.
And the mystery
Sang alive
Still in the water and singingbirds.

And there could I marvel my birthday
Away but the weather turned around. And the true
Joy of the long dead child sang burning
In the sun.
It was my thirtieth
Year to heaven stood there then in the summer noon
Though the town below lay leaved with October blood.
O may my heart's truth
Still be sung
On this high hill in a year's turning.

Dylan Thomas

"As with all affinities it seems I've known and loved Dylan Thomas' poetry all my life. Last year, talking with my nephew Ben I tried to explain what moves me so much about paint and this peom sprang to mind, in particular the stanza, which contains the sublime phrase '. . . the parables of sunlight . . .' "

1. Untitled 1994 oil The Hunting Art Prizes London 1995 first prize – private collection

With many works of art, what you see is what you get. Unmistakably, it is a specific landscape, the portrait or bust of a person or an arrangement of known objects. Most people are comfortable with this and it is, perhaps, why many are uneasy when faced with abstract paintings or sculptures. They offer no apparent subject, no reassurance that the artist has manifested his or her ability to represent accurately or feelingly what is depicted. Such ambiguity can be discomfiting.

Mary Griffiths chooses not to title her works, even though they are clearly representational. The viewer faced with group paintings in her 2002 exhibition ". . . the parables of sunlight . . ." may well ask: "What is that man pointing at?" or "Why are these people gathered here?" Lacking direction from Griffiths, it would be an unimaginative onlooker who did not instinctively start to provide a possible explanation for what is happening. Mary welcomes this.

"I love ambiguity in pictures. Most of my big paintings are narratives, which I deliberately do not title because this allows people to contribute something to what they see. I have seen so many people look at the captions on the wall before they look at the painting, to substantiate what it is that they are looking at. I want to say to them: 'Give yourself permission to see what you wish to see in it, and then look at the caption if you wish to.' By not titling, I am giving the viewer a chance to bring his or her body of experience to a work. The thing I like about exhibiting is that you do get an enormous feedback."

"I have had interpretations of my paintings that I have never thought of, which is exciting. Sometimes, what has been said is so pertinent that I have taken it away with me into another painting. When I won the Hunting competition, the works were on show in Swansea. A man came up to my group painting and said: 'I know who these people are. They're steel workers from Llanelli, aren't they?' I thought, how *wonderful*. It is a reading that I would never have given it, although it was perfectly sound, and made sense."

It is not surprising that some have said that Griffiths' work has religious overtones. She finds that gratifying. When asked to paint to the theme Via Crucis for the Millennium 2000 show at Chappel Galleries, she was delighted. "I found it very easy to work to that theme. It is so much a part of our culture. It is everywhere. Everybody knows, say, the works of Rembrandt and Rubens, the classic Stations of Cross, and so on. In a sense, of course, it was almost too daunting. What could I contribute to all that?"

With her 2002 show, she has returned from universally recognised subjects to the anonymous. Soon, questions pose themselves. Who *are* these people who populate her enigmatic pictures? Why are they so disposed on the canvas? And to what extent were these quite ambitiously large pictures planned before she picked up her brush?

"It would be wrong to think that the final picture is what I had in mind when I started. It is a truism to say that all painting is abstract, since it is essentially mark-making. Now that I am fortunate to work in a big space, it makes sense to explore working on a larger scale. I have never worked on this scale before."

Contributing to the element of ambiguity in Griffiths' group pictures is the way that the separate characters relate to each other. They are, in fact, individual portraits composed on to the canvas. "Sometimes I do preliminary drawings, sometimes I paint from life, sometimes from photographs. It is a mix. The working process is an extraordinary thing, unique to each painter. I could never do what Stanley Spencer did: draw, square the drawing up, square up the canvas, then paint systematically from left to right."

"For me, a white canvas is daunting. So I like to put a lot of spontaneous marks down, then build up – an accretion of intentions, intentions thwarted, mistakes, and so on. I think it would bore me to work more systematically." Underlying this method is "the set of intentions that I bring to the canvas. Sometimes, the picture will flow. At other times I reach a sort of impasse, where I am not sure what to do next. All this offers me the maximum opportunity of surprise. I don't like to do anything by rote. What I find exciting about painting is that you are bringing order out of chaos, or trying to. There is a tension between the two. It is no accident that down the ages one of the abiding motifs of Western painting is Jacob wrestling with the angel. It is a classic metaphor for what painting is like."

"There are parallels with religion. You have very dark moments when you think: 'I don't know that I can do this.' It should be the case that where you have a long track record, painting becomes easier. But it doesn't. It is still an act of faith, where you hope that if you are persistent and dogged enough, you will come through."

Does she ever give up the struggle? "No, I never abandon a painting. I put it to one side and begin something else. Every time that I enter the studio

I may not be conscious of the unfinished picture, but it is in the corner of my eye. Invariably, one day, while intending to continue work on the current picture, you realise what the set to one side one needs and you carry on with it. It is organic, and that is the way that all my paintings evolve. I can live with paintings for years, and even when I think I have finished them I could go on with them."

Ideas crowd in faster than Griffiths can paint them. The door of the studio may have been closed, but pictures are still with her when, say, walking down the street. It is in such public places that she has found many of her models.

"I am a people-watcher. I find people compelling. The other day I saw an old dear, coming back with her shopping, who had on a coat of a colour complimentary to her skin tones. I thought: "How I would love to paint you!" Sometimes, I will ask people if I can. Invariably, their reaction is generous. Beauty comes in all shapes and sizes. I especially like older people, whose history, like trees, can be read in their forms."

Occasionally she will pay models, although for most artists this is an expensive option. "For a time I ran a life drawing group in Cambridge, where I live, and we all chipped in to pay the model. I tax models to the hilt, but invariably: 'Models become friends and friends models.' "

Griffiths is unusual in that she has forged a career as a professional artist without resorting to regular teaching, which while providing income can, for many, sap the creative energies. Her own hard-won experience has made her sceptical about conventional art school training. "I don't accept I've ever been trained and feel very much self-taught, but fundamentally I think this is true of most artists. After all, what any artist is attempting to do is articulate his or her individual way of saying 'Hallelujah'. At first you may ape a style, but as you progress you absorb and assimilate and forge your own distinctive voice. What was valuable about the experience of art college is that it enabled me to meet like-minded people such as John Bellany, Gus Cummins and Bruce McLean, who opened up my horizons as to what was possible. When I went to art college in the 1970s, nobody was teaching anybody effectively."

One of Griffiths' strengths as an artist is her ability to draw. Here, she acknowledges a debt to her mother. She had been thwarted from taking up a grammar school scholarship for lack of money, also wanted to be an artist and had a wonderful drawing ability. While in London during the war training to be a nurse, she familiarised herself with the art galleries, and grew to appreciate the Old Masters.

Later, having married and settled back in Wales with her husband, a white-collar worker in the steel industry, on London visits she would take her family to see what she had appreciated. Mary's brother and sister were soon bored, "but when I saw the Holbein drawings at Windsor my eyes nearly popped out of my head. It was like I had been wanting something without knowing what it was. When I saw the Holbeins, I knew that was it. Even now, I still think they are some of the best things produced on the planet."

Mary also acknowledges the influence of Dorothy Daniel, her art teacher at Llanelli Girls' Grammar School. Domestic circumstances had dictated that Daniel, a prizewinner at the Slade School of Fine Art, famed for its teaching of drawing, had ended up in the classroom at Llanelli, a post for which she was over-qualified. "I loved her, because she was so enabling," Mary says. "She would bring in her own work, abstract, with beautiful colour, and would lend me her own art books. I would see things for the first time that were so exciting."

Now, as well as the Old Masters, Griffiths has a catholic appreciation of modern painters, from Lucian Freud to Patrick Heron and Ronald Kitaj, from Prunella Clough to Käthe Kollwitz. It is not surprising that among the tops for her is that singular artist Roger Hilton, with his whiplash, quixotic line, another very different Slade-trained draughtsman. "I always seek out Hilton's work. I think that everything he did was marvellous. He is awesome, and his risk-taking is audacious. It is knife-edge stuff that either works or it doesn't."

"The drawings of Frank Auerbach are very important to me, because they're so fearless and so tender. It's a very difficult thing to bring off successfully. I think I value those two qualities more than any others and one without the other isn't good enough."

It was 1987, nine years after she left art college, before Griffiths began to show her work in solo and mixed exhibitions. On reflection, this seems odd in one so single-minded who has since become a prolific exhibitor and who has gathered an impressive string of commendations and prizes. The missing years were not, however, fallow ones. "I was always working if not exhibiting, then in 1987 I was ready to exhibit, with a body of pictures to show."

After college she spent some time in Aberystwyth, returned to London because of the need to know what was going on in the visual arts, then moved to Cambridge where friends were, and has stayed. She concedes that to be a full-time artist is "a very privileged way of living." It has, however, been a hard-earned privilege, founded on years of hardship, self-belief and "a stubborn streak" that would not admit defeat in the battle for self-fulfilment.

Now, her routine is to be in the studio around nine o'clock in the morning, painting on until she elects to go. "The winters exasperate me! I *can* paint by artificial light, but that means moving on to other paintings, because otherwise you can't get the tones and artificial light demands a different palette. I can't bear interruption, and I am very mean with my time. I don't think you can be a serious painter unless you do a 10- or 12-hour stint a day, however innately gifted you are. Sometimes it's difficult, but that's part of the nature of the challenge."

If she finds painting frustrating, she can discover satisfaction in drawing. Most difficult to attempt are those in the manner of Hilton, where the model is depicted in a few lines. "For every drawing of that sort that works, you probably have to throw away a dozen that don't. What is satisfying is to say all you have to say as economically as possible. Then, it is a pure joy."

Those who have observed Griffith's work over the years will have perceived the presence of a number of influences and themes. Some, like the influence of Gauguin on her 1992 BP Portrait Award entry, are temporary. One theme, that of procession, in all shapes and sizes, seems to have lasted forever. Early memories contributed to its germination. "When I was a child in Llanelli I would dreamily make pictures in my head out of anything. We lived on the main thoroughfare to the rugby pitch, to which seemingly endless people would gravitate. Maybe such processions are a metaphor for life, with no beginning and no end."

"Look at the work of Matisse, who has long been one of my passions. Do you know his swimming pool, which runs around an entire room? I am beguiled by this idea. For years I have worked on panels and I would like to create a ribbon of them right around, say, the walls of the Chappel Galleries, an endless procession. I don't know how you would sell it, but the concept is tremendously exciting."

DAVID BUCKMAN

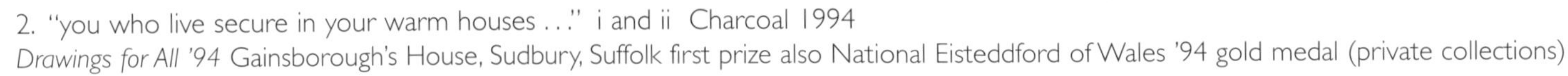

2. "you who live secure in your warm houses . . ." i and ii Charcoal 1994
Drawings for All '94 Gainsborough's House, Sudbury, Suffolk first prize also National Eisteddford of Wales '94 gold medal (private collections)

LIST OF PLATES

3. John oil on panel 14 x 12.5cm

4. Untitled oil on panel 15 x 13.5cm

5. Untitled pencil and gouache 17 x 13cm

6. Untitled pencil and gouache 14 x 11cm

7. At the Lido oil on panel 61 x 91cm

8. Tim
oil on panel
23 x 19cm

9. Untitled oil on panel 18 x 16cm

10. Untitled oil on paper 57 x 59cm

11. Untitled oil on canvas 87 x 137cm

12. Untitled oil on panel 34 x 24.5cm

13. Johnny oil on canvas 52 x 36cm

14. Untitled oil on panel 47 x 42cm

15. Untitled
oil on panel
47 x 42cm

16. Hugh oil on panel 15x 14cm

17. Malcolm oil on panel 28 x 20cm

18. Procession oil on panel 30 x 60cm

19. Procession oil on paper 26.5 x 59cm

20. Untitled oil on panel 29 × 22cm

21. Untitled oil on panel 30 x 20cm

22. Untitled pencil and gouache 17.5 × 12.5cm

23. Untitled pencil and gouache 15 × 14.5cm

24. Daniel oil on panel 19.5 x 15cm

25. Study for in the Park oil on paper 64 x 25cm

26. Untitled oil on panel 23 x 19cm

27. Untitled pencil on paper 51x 34cm

MARY GRIFFITHS

1956 Born Wales
1974-75 Dyfed College of Art
1975-78 Croydon College of Art
Taught by John Bellany R.A., Bruce McLean and Gus Cummins
2000 Member of Royal Cambrian Academy
(invited by Sir Kyffin Williams RA)

SOLO SHOWS:

1987 ADC Theatre, Park St., Cambridge
1988 Clare College, Cambridge
1989 Thaxted Festival
1991 St. John's Gallery, Bury St. Edmunds
1993/95/97/00/02 Chappel Galleries, Colchester
1998 Martin Tinney Gallery, Cardiff
2001 Martin Tinney Gallery, Cardiff

MIXED SHOWS:

1987/88/92/93/94/97/99
Eastern Open, King's Lynn, Norfolk
1987 Oast Room Gallery, Cambridge
1988/94 'Drawings For All', Gainsborough's House, Sudbury and Regional Tour
1989/94 Haylett's Gallery, Colchester
1990 'The Drawing Show', Contact Gallery, Norwich
1990 Royal Society of Portrait Painters, Mall Galleries, London
1990 Royal Society of British Artists, London
1990 Singer & Friedlander/*Sunday Times* Watercolour Competition, London and Glasgow
1990 New Gallery, Swansea
1991/94/95/97 Bow House Gallery, Barnet, London
1991 'Modern Contemporaries', Chappel Galleries, Essex
1992-97 Chappel Galleries, Essex
1991 'Britain's Painter', Westminster Galleries, London
1992 BP National Portrait Competition, National Portrait Gallery, London
1992 'The Human Form', Conservatory Gallery, Cambridge
1993 Leicestershire Art Collection
1993/94 Royal National Eisteddfod of Wales
1994/95 Hunting Art Prize, R.C.A. London
1994 Spring Collection, East West Gallery, London
1994 Wales Art Fair, Cardiff
1995 'Drawing Near' – Touring Show, Fife
1995 Hunting Art Prizes: R.C.A. London and Swansea
1995 'Making a Mark', Mall Galleries, London
1995 'Showcase Wales', Y Tabernacl, M.O.M.A. Wales
1995/96 Martin Tinney Gallery, Cardiff
1995/96 John Martin Gallery, London
1997 'On A Grand Scale', John Martin Gallery, London
1996/97/98/99/00 Art Fair, Islington, London
1996 'The Human Form', Mall Galleries, London
1996 'Human Interest', Bury St. Edmunds Art Gallery
1996 Conservatory Gallery, Cambridge
1996/97/98 Langham Fine Art, Bury St. Edmunds
1996 Guest: Royal Society of British Artists
1996 Poetry Commission, Prospero Poets, Clarion Press
1996 The Gallery, Cork St., London
1997 Chelsea Art Fair, London
1997 Contemporary Welsh Art, Hong Kong
1999 Martin Tinney Gallery at Cork St, London
2000 British Art Fair, London
'Gold Medal Winners' Exhibition, National Eisteddfod'
2001 Royal National Eisteddfod of Wales
Langham Fine Art, Bury St. Edmunds
Royal Cambrian Academy Summer Show
Martin Tinney Gallery at Cork St., London

PRIZES:

1988 Lady Evershed Drawing Prize, Eastern Open
1991 Highly Commended, Britain's Painters, London
1992 Highly Commended – Painting, Eastern Open
1993 Highly Commended – Drawing, Eastern Open
1994 Highly Commended – Hunting Competition
1994 First Prize, 'Drawings For All', Suffolk
1994 Gold Medal in Fine Art, National Eisteddfod of Wales
1995 First Prize, Hunting Art Prizes, R.C.A. London
1997 Lady Evershed Drawing Prize, Eastern Open
1999 Painting Prize, Eastern Open